D0854898

ROBERT FULTON

DISCOVER THE LIFE OF AN INVENTOR

Don McLeese

Rourke Publishing LLC
Vero Beach, Florida 32964

© 2006 Rourke Publishing LLC

All rights reserved. No part of this book may be reproduced or utilized in any form or by any means, electronic or mechanical including photocopying, recording, or by any information storage and retrieval system without permission in writing from the publisher.

www.rourkepublishing.com

PHOTO CREDITS: Cover, pg 18 ©Getty Images; pg 21 courtesy of The Delta Queen Steamboat Company; All other images from the Library of Congress

Title page: *A Hudson River steamboat from the 1850s*

Library of Congress Cataloging-in-Publication Data

McLeese, Don.
  Robert Fulton / Don McLeese.
     p. cm. -- (Discover the life of an inventor II)
  Includes bibliographical references and index.
  ISBN 1-59515-434-5 (hardcover)
 1. Fulton, Robert, 1765-1815--Juvenile literature. 2. Marine engineers--United States--Biography--Juvenile literature. 3. Inventors--United States--Biography--Juvenile literature. 4. Steamboats--United states--History--19th century--Juvenile literature. I. Title.
  VM140.F9M385 2006
  623.82'4'092--dc22
                                        2005011434

Printed in the USA

Rourke Publishing
1-800-394-7055
www.rourkepublishing.com
sales@rourkepublishing.com
Post Office Box 3328, Vero Beach, FL 32964

TABLE OF CONTENTS

DID HE OR DIDN'T HE?

Robert Fulton is famous for being the man who invented the **steamboat**. But did he? There were boats powered by **steam** before Fulton made one. But his was the one that was most popular. His steamboat was big enough to hold 50 people and safe enough so that it wouldn't rock or sink in the water.

Steamboats were a very popular way to travel, as shown here at St. Louis.

BORN IN PENNSYLVANIA

Robert was born on November 14, 1765. His family lived in Lancaster County in what is now the state of Pennsylvania. The United States didn't become a country until 1776.

Robert's father was also named Robert. He had come to America from Ireland. Robert's mother was named Mary. Robert had three older sisters and one younger brother.

American colonists declared their freedom from the British in 1776.

A POOR FAMILY

Robert's family didn't have a lot of money. His father tried farming, but he couldn't grow anything so he sold the farm. When Robert was only nine years old, his father died. It was hard for Robert's mother to support the family and raise five children on her own.

Robert Fulton
1806

GROWING UP

When Robert was a boy, he loved to paint pictures. People told him that being an artist would be a hard way to make a living. Robert also liked to **invent** things.

Fulton built a **paddle wheel** for a rowboat. The paddle wheel operated by hand and was easier than rowing the boat. He sketched plans for a **submarine**. He also built an air rifle. Fulton wanted to learn how things worked, and he wanted to make new things.

Among other ideas, Fulton sketched plans for a submarine, shown here above and under the water.

MOVE TO THE CITY

When he was only 17, Robert moved to Philadelphia. This was the biggest city in Pennsylvania. There Robert became friends with a man who would become very famous: Benjamin Franklin. Robert continued to draw and paint. He also drew plans for different machines and inventions.

Benjamin Franklin addresses an assembly in London on behalf of the American colonies.

ON TO ENGLAND

When Robert was 21, he went to live in London, England. Benjamin Franklin had friends there and asked them to help Robert.

Fulton continued to paint pictures and to draw plans. He became very interested in boats on canals and the bridges over them.

While he was living in England, Fulton began working on designs for bridges and canals.

FROM SUBMARINES TO STEAMBOATS

Robert became interested in all sorts of boats. In 1797, he traveled to France and began working with a submarine.

While he was there, the American **ambassador** to France asked him to help make a steamboat. Robert was very interested in the idea of a boat powered by steam. Other inventors had **experimented** with such boats, but they hadn't worked well.

In France, Fulton showed steamboat plans to Napoleon Bonaparte.

BACK TO THE UNITED STATES

In 1806, Robert returned to the United States. He built a steamboat, which he called the *Clermont.* In 1807, the *Clermont* made its first trip on the Hudson River, from New York City to Albany. It soon was making regular trips carrying passengers, the first steamboat to do this. Robert's steamboat was a big success!

An illustration of the Clermont
in New York's harbor

A FAMOUS INVENTOR

The steamboat made Robert Fulton famous. He was only 49 years old when he died on February 23, 1815. Almost 200 years later, when people think of steamboats, they remember Robert Fulton.

The Mississippi Queen *is a modern version of the steamboat.*

IMPORTANT DATES TO REMEMBER

1765   Robert Fulton is born

1782   Robert moves to Philadelphia at age 17

1786   Robert moves to London and works on designing canals and bridges

1797   Robert travels to France and works on a submarine

1806   Robert returns to the United States and builds a steamboat

1807   Robert's steamboat, the *Clermont,* makes its first trip

1815   Robert Fulton dies at the age of 49

GLOSSARY

ambassador (am BAS uh dur) — someone sent by the government of one country to deal with the government of another country

experimented (ek SPARE uh ment ud) — to have tested something, to have tried something out

invent (in VENT) — make something new that no one has ever made before

paddle wheel (PAD ul WHEEL) — a wheel with paddles used to propel a boat

steam (STEEM) — what water becomes, a gas (or vapor) that produces energy when it is heated

steamboat (STEEM BOT) — a boat powered by heating water until it becomes steam

submarine (SUB muh REEN) — a ship designed for underwater travel

INDEX

Further Reading

Ford, Carin T. *Robert Fulton: The Steamboat Man.* Enslow Publishers, 2004

Gillis, Jennifer Blizin. *Robert Fulton.* Heinemann, 2004

Websites to Visit

http://www.robertfulton.org/

http://en.wikipedia.org/wiki/Robert_Fulton

About the Author

Don McLeese is an associate professor of journalism at the University of Iowa. He has won many awards for his journalism, and his work has appeared in numerous newspapers and magazines. He has written many books for young readers. He lives with his wife and two daughters in West Des Moines, Iowa.

WITHDRAWN
HOWARD COUNTY LIBRARY